45, 35, NOW.....THE CONTINUUM OF ISLAM IN AMERICA

Examining the Evolution of the Islamic Experience in 21st Century America

Amin Nathari

45, 35, Now…..The Continuum of Islam in America

Sabree Press
P O Box 25257
Newark, NJ 07101

© 2011, Q. Amin Nathari
(2nd printing – October 2011)
All Rights Reserved.

ISBN 978-1-887513-05-0

Website: www.aminnathari.com

45, 35, Now…..The Continuum of Islam in America

Introduction   4

45:

February 21, 1965 – The assassination of Malcolm X, also known as El-Hajj Malik Shabazz (May 19, 1925 – February 21, 1965)   13

35:

February 25, 1975 – The passing of Elijah Muhammad (October 7, 1897 – February 25, 1975)   22

February 26, 1975 – Wallace D. Muhammad is the new leader of the Nation of Islam   32

25 after 35:

February 25 - 27, 2000 – Saviour's Day weekend and the public reunion of Imam W. Deen Mohammed and Minister Louis Farrakhan   42

Now…..The Continuum of Islam in America

September 9, 2008 – The passing of Imam W. Deen Mohammed (October 30, 1933 – September 9, 2008)   50

A New Way Forward for the 21st Century   59

Final Thoughts   78

About the Author   88

About IAM – the Islam in America Movement   90

45, 35, Now…..The Continuum of Islam in America

Introduction

A little more than ten years ago, in June 2001, I wrote a relatively short paper which was later published as a booklet, titled *From "the Nation" to "the Sunnah": Building the Bridge in 21st Century America.* It was originally intended to be the first paper in a series documenting the phenomena of the steady growth of Islam in America, and the large number of people, predominately African-Americans, reverting to Islam after being members of the group and dynamic organization known as the Nation of Islam (NOI). At the time, which was a little more than one year removed from the February 26, 2000 25th anniversary of the beginning of the transition of the Nation of Islam, I felt that this issue, unique to the Muslim American experience, certainly required analysis and thought, particularly in light of the then-expected continued growth trend of Islam in America, and the present composition of the Muslim Community at the time. Of course, I had no idea how in just a few short months, with the tragic events of September 11, 2001, the landscape of Muslim America would be even further impacted.

Even in its limited distribution, I received encouraging feedback from the paper, and many expressed appreciation at my

45, 35, Now.....The Continuum of Islam in America

treatment of the subject. Rather than increase distribution of the published booklet, I decided at that moment to focus on other contemporary research and upon the next landmark date, 30 years after the transition which would be 2005. My thinking was I would gather together historians, scholars and others interested in this subject and convene a forum, or symposium of sorts. Well, the Creator is certainly the Best of Planners. The year 2005 found my life in an entirely different place and space, and our community busy with other challenges, goals and objectives. In late 2004 I had written a book titled *Muslim Unity By Any Means Necessary* and during most of 2005 I traveled throughout the country lecturing on the book and along the way, addressing the 30 year transition theme among other topics.

However, the following year, 2006, after completing work on the mayoral campaign of newly elected mayor Cory A. Booker and the municipal council campaigns of some of the members of his team in Newark, NJ, and subsequently beginning what would be a 13 month stint as Deputy Director of Communications for the City of Newark, my birthplace and hometown, I made a firm commitment to do either one of the following: in February 2010 I would convene a symposium, as previously mentioned, to be themed: *45, 35, Now*; or I would wait even further and in February 2015 convene the same

45, 35, Now…..The Continuum of Islam in America

symposium to be themed *50, 40, Now*. To borrow a phrase often used by President Barack Obama during his campaign, *the fierce urgency of now*, and not being so presumptuous as to think I had an assurance *until* 2015 motivated me to direct my energies into what became known as *45, 35, Now…..The Continuum of Islam in America*. When we began advertising and promoting the symposium, which took place over two days at the historic Philadelphia Masjid – Sister Clara Muhammad School on February 19-20, 2010, one of the most often asked questions was "what does 45, 35, Now represent?" Well, as I did then, please allow me to explain:

The year 2010 marked the "anniversary" of two watershed, defining moments in not just Black American history, but the history of America itself; *45* years ago, on February 21, 1965, the assassination of Malcolm X, and *35* years ago, February 25, 1975, the death of Elijah Muhammad, leader of the Nation of Islam (NOI) and the subsequent ascension of his son (the late) Imam W. Deen Mohammed (then known as Wallace D. Muhammad) as leader of the NOI. The latter event was the catalyst for what is widely considered to be the largest influx of Americans accepting and embracing *traditional* or often referred to as *Sunni* Islam, (meaning the understanding and practice of Islam based on the sacred text of the Qur'an and the

45, 35, Now…..The Continuum of Islam in America

Sunnah or Prophetic Tradition of the Prophet Muhammad, prayers and peace be upon him (pbuh) and by most, the largest mass religious "conversion" in American history. This book, *45, 35, Now…..The Continuum of Islam in America (Examining the Evolution of the Islamic Experience in 21st Century America)*, is the humble outcome of my assessment of that reality.

My objective in this concise work is to examine what I feel to be key events and happenings, both in the historical development and contemporary reality of Muslims and the Islamic Experience in America, in relationship to the periods of time mentioned. The occurrence of the two landmark events of the title are of particular importance, as they helped direct the course of *Muslim America*. Among the other important events included in this chronology are the February 27, 2000 public reunion of Imam W. Deen Mohammed and Minister Louis Farrakhan, and the September 9, 2008 passing of the visionary leader Imam W. Deen Mohammed.

By no means is this to be considered the definitive text on the topic, or an exhaustive undertaking of research and rigorous academic strivings. It is a historical narrative, also anchored and enriched by the first-hand account of myself and others who

45, 35, Now…..The Continuum of Islam in America

have been, what I consider as, fortunate enough to have lived through and experienced most and in many cases all of the events and time periods reflected in this work. I hope my analysis and observations will be used to outline new, contemporary perspectives, both to those engaged in research on Islam and Muslims in America, as well as to the American public, amongst whom Islam culturally and otherwise enriches and Muslims continue to live and contribute. I pray that future historians will give this subject the trenchant examination and full treatment it truly deserves.

Twenty-first century America, dubbed the New Millennium in popular circles, has found the Islamic experience at a pivotal crossroads. Islam, the world's fastest growing religion and way of life, is further solidifying its presence within the American landscape. A report called *"The Mosque in America: A National Portrait"*, a major study of the Muslim Community in the United States released on April 26, 2001, supported conservative estimates of a total Muslim American population of seven million. Although more recent studies have seemed to reduce this number substantially, I opt to use the data from the 2001 report as a more accurate barometer of the current numbers.

45, 35, Now.....The Continuum of Islam in America

This report, and the findings of similar reports based upon other research conducted, also mentions that many of the Muslims in America, nearly 30%, are converts, or as often referred to within the Muslim community, *reverts,* particularly in the case of African-Americans, many of whose ancestors were Muslims when brought here to America as slaves. Additionally, the report also confirms that by conservative estimates, 30% of members of the average mosque are African-American.

It also must be noted that the majority of the mosques in America are also relatively young; 30% of all mosques were established in the 1990's and 32% were founded in the 1980's. My own research, again supported by the research studies of others, indicates that the vast majority of these mosques founded in the 1980's were the direct result of the first transition from the Nation of Islam that began in 1975. Therefore, it can be accurately concluded that a substantial number of Muslim African-Americans today have either directly transitioned from, or otherwise been influenced by the Nation of Islam, both as it existed up until 1975, and today, as it currently exists under the leadership and direction of Minister Louis Farrakhan.

45, 35, Now…..The Continuum of Islam in America

I am not asserting that all African-American reverts or converts to Islam came by way of the Nation of Islam. History will record, has already recorded, and I certainly acknowledge and give credit and respect to the work of the many forerunners, those who blazed the trail of *Sunni-Islam* with varying degrees of success, when the correct, traditional practicing of Islam and being Muslim in America was not popular, as we find it is today. The works and legacies of Professor Muhammad Ezaldeen, Imam Wali Akram, Hajj Heshaam Jaaber, just to name a few, and may Allah have Mercy on all of them, not to mention the early existence of some of the immigrant organizations, are a testament to the existence of Islam in America outside of the confines of the Nation of Islam.

However, I maintain that in order for an accurate and objective analysis to be done around the current state of Islam in America, particularly as it relates to the African-American community, it is imperative that we examine the chain of events that help set the stage for what exists today. These events and occurrences left an indelible imprint upon the landscape of Islam in America; it would be prudent for us to assess it, as objectively and pragmatically as possible, extracting from it the valuable lessons contained therein, and perhaps, build upon the best practices that are reflected as well.

45, 35, Now…..The Continuum of Islam in America

A final note: having already acknowledged as fact that not all Muslim Americans, African-American or immigrant, entered into Islam or lived the experience of the Nation of Islam, my ardent hope is to engage, in addition to the general audience noted earlier, two distinct and particular categories or groups of Muslim Americans: my immigrant brothers and sisters of many ethnicities and cultures who came to America from various places throughout the world, and certainly the second (and subsequent) generation(s) that were born from them; and African-American Muslims that did *not* enter into Islam via the Nation of Islam, including those that accepted in what I refer to as *post-transition* after 1975.

My humble yet extensive and varied experience as a Muslim grassroots worker, community servant and other roles over my lifetime thus far, has illustrated to me the importance, in fact I consider it a necessity, for these two groups to better understand the Islamic evolution of those who have lived and experienced the reality of the periods covered in this book. Although Muslims share a common faith and are united, bonded by the sacred text, prophetic tradition and the basic beliefs and tenets of the religion and way of life of Islam, our cultural, political, social and other influences and upbringing leaves an indelible imprint upon us, thus shaping our historic and contemporary realities. This is particularly important to bear in mind and consider with regards to defining, establishing and implementing the agenda for *the Muslim American Community*.

I deliberately used that term with emphasis, as this community is a broad, diverse and expansive collection of many aspirations, goals, interests and objectives. What may be priority number one for a particular segment of the community might very well be number ten on the list of priorities for another segment, even within the same geographical area. I assert that it is through the mutual understanding of the varied paths that have blazed the trail of Islam in America that more effective working relationships can be developed and nurtured; and the ideal of what I have been referring to for a number of years now, *functional unity*, can and will become the goal and the standard as we collectively live the continuum of Islam in 21st Century America. If this modest narrative helps to make any progress towards that noble objective, then I will have fulfilled my intention and consider this effort a *success*. And all success is from and all credit belongs to Allah, Lord of all the Worlds; only the mistakes have been mine.

Amin Nathari
August 2011
Newark, NJ USA

45, 35, Now.....The Continuum of Islam in America

45: February 21, 1965 – the assassination of Malcolm X, also known as Al-Hajj Malik Shabazz
May 19, 1925 – February 21, 1965

On this date, at the Audubon Ballroom in the village of Harlem, in New York City, the man born as Malcolm Little and known to the world as Malcolm X was gunned down by assassins' bullets. There exist numerous books and other media about the assassination, consisting both of known facts as well as possibilities and theories. What is known and indisputable is that Malcolm X was killed at the age of 39, a few months shy of his 40th birthday.

In addition to the famous book *The Autobiography of Malcolm X* (as told to Alex Haley), a plethora of works exist around the biography, philosophy, evolution and other aspects of the life of this complex, iconic figure, among them includes books by Peter Goldman, Bruce Perry and most recently, a comprehensive and in some circles controversial new biography by the scholar Manning Marable, who passed away just a few days before the release of the book. For the purposes of this work, I focus briefly on the role of Malcolm X as National Spokesman for the Nation of Islam until March 1964, and how

45, 35, Now…..The Continuum of Islam in America

his assassination less than a year later began a pivotal ten year period that would change the course of Islam in America.

The evolution of the man born as Malcolm Little from Detroit Red, petty criminal and hustler to Malcolm X is well chronicled and documented. According to his autobiography, while in prison in 1947, two of Malcolm's brothers encouraged him to learn about the teachings of the Honorable Elijah Muhammad. After Malcolm was paroled in 1952, he expressed his dissatisfaction about what he felt as too few people attending the Nation of Islam Detroit Temple #1. Immediately he went to work. The next year Elijah Muhammad would appoint him as minister at the Detroit Temple. Over the following three years Malcolm would establish temples in major cities such as New York (#7), Boston (#11) and Philadelphia (#12). He quickly rose to prominence within the NOI, and utilizing his charismatic and dynamic speaking style along with grassroots engagement, he became the Nation's most able and well-known representative.

Transcending the role of *Temple Minister*, Malcolm was an active and frequent speaker within the broader community, especially on his *home turf* in Harlem, and he was one of the most sought after speakers on college and university campuses

45, 35, Now.....The Continuum of Islam in America

throughout America. And during the nearly 12 years that he served as a minister under Elijah Muhammad, the Nation continued to grow by leaps and bounds. Through Malcolm's representation many would come to be attracted to the Nation, and a few would join and go on to ultimately become famous themselves, most notably a former Calypso singer known as *the Charmer*, Louis Walcott, later to be known as Louis Farrakhan and certainly not the least, a brash but talented young boxer named Cassius Clay, later known to the world as Muhammad Ali.

A number of factors, also well documented, among them internal differences within the NOI, personal jealousies and conflicting agendas, Malcolm's own continued ideological evolution, his frustration with the NOI's policy of socio-political non-engagement, and not the least of all, the involvement and interference on the part of the US intelligence community, resulted in the December 4, 1963 suspension of Malcolm X from his national spokesperson duties, and his silencing for what was understood to be a period of 90 days. Events that would transpire over that period of time, exacerbated by the same factors mentioned, made it clear that Malcolm would never be able to serve in the capacity that he previously had or as effectively as he did prior to his suspension.

On March 8, 1964 Malcolm X announced that he was leaving the Nation of Islam, and four days later at the Park Sheraton Hotel in New York City he outlined what would be the start of his new direction, post-NOI. Before proceeding with an examination, albeit a brief one, of what would be Malcolm's direction during the 11 months to follow until his tragic assassination, it is important to note the time, place and context within which this is occurring. Although immigrants had been in America prior to this time, 1965 would bring the *Immigration and Nationality Act*, abolishing the *National Origins Formula* that had been in effect in the US since the *Immigration Act of 1924*. This legislation effectively paved the way for a non-quota based, less stringent immigration system, more widespread legal immigration, and resulted in the beginning of a mass influx of immigrants from what could be popularly referred to as *the Muslim world*, vis-à-vis, the Middle East. This, in addition to the *Civil Rights Act of 1964*, (enacted July 2, 1964), that outlawed major forms of discrimination against blacks and women, including racial segregation, would have the potential to ultimately change the landscape of race relations in the US.

45, 35, Now…..The Continuum of Islam in America

As early as 1959, Malcolm was introduced to *Sunni*-Islam while serving as an ambassador of the NOI in preparation for Elijah Muhammads' planned Umrah (out of season pilgrimage to Mecca). It was in this same year, 1959 that several mainstream Islamic groups and organizations began to question and in some cases openly launch attacks on the Islamic legitimacy of the NOI and more specifically, Elijah Muhammad and his bona-fides as a Muslim. Malcolm frequently did verbal and written battle with these critics, oftentimes even citing passages from the Qur'an in an attempt to legitimize many aspects of the NOI's doctrine and to quell the criticisms.

Yet as the 1960s began, we see that Malcolm began to be challenged even more, and at the same time while being exposed to more information about Islam, we gradually see his perspectives start to change and evolve. According to his autobiography, his intimate conversations and contacts with *Sunni*-Muslims were increasing, and among his many interactions with immigrant Muslims (whom were often referred to as *foreigners* in the NOI) it was Dr. Mahmoud Youssef Shawarbi, a University of Cairo Professor in the United States teaching at Fordham University on a Fulbright scholarship that encouraged Malcolm to make the hajj, (pilgrimage to Mecca) and instructed and assisted him with the basic concepts of Islam as practiced by the then one billion plus Muslims around the world at that time. Again, this is very important to bear in mind as we continue.

"I am and will always be a Muslim".

This was among the many statements that Malcolm would make on March 12, 1964, as he outlined his new direction. "I'm going to organize and head a mosque in New York City". He said that this was necessary as Islam "gives us the spiritual force necessary to rid our people of the vices that destroy the moral fiber of our community". In subsequent speeches in the weeks to follow it would become clear that Malcolm firmly believed as he said on March 18, 1964 at Harvard College "the religion of Islam combined with Black Nationalism is all that is needed to solve the problem of the Black community".

With this in mind and taking into account his post-Hajj activities and work, I argue that although Malcolm saw much beauty and hope in the universal brotherhood of Islam, he did not see it as a means of avoidance when it came to addressing the aspirations, goals and hopes of his people, specifically, African-Americans. I have stated in a previous work, and on many occasions when discussing the issue, Malcolm did not see Islam as a passport out of *Blackness*. I offer that he was continuing to search for a way to bridge the gap, to connect the two, Black Nationalism and *Sunni*-Islam, even if it meant appropriating some of the best practices of the very Nation of Islam that he had just separated from. This is certainly understandable, given his *Garveyite* upbringing and the similarities that organization shared with the NOI.

During the months leading up to his assassination, Malcolm toured Africa, forging relationships with leaders throughout the continent, while at the same time entangled in a legal battle with the NOI over ownership of the home he and his family still lived in. During his time in Africa, Malcolm would become even more influenced by Pan-Africanism, and this would seemingly form the basis of Malcolm's liberation strategy; yet while this was the driving force behind his politics, he never cast aside his own commitment to, and interest in, Islam.

After Malcolm's departure from the NOI many of its detractors predicted its demise. It was argued that absent the charisma of Malcolm, combined with its nonexistent relationship with the civil rights establishment and the increasing attacks against its Islamic legitimacy, the Nation of Islam could not, and would not survive. Some historians, observers and other social scientists present this as an argument to support why the NOI would have certainly been supported of, and most likely behind the assassination of Malcolm. And certainly the rhetoric spewed by some of its ministers contributed to the climate that led to Malcolm's assassination, thus, supporting that argument.

What is also well known, yet in my opinion, given little attention in the academic community, is that the ten year period following the assassination of Malcolm X up until the February 25, 1975 passing of Elijah Muhammad was the most productive period of growth and development in the Nation of Islam's history. During the height of the 1960's Civil Rights movement and transitioning into the 1970s Black Power movement, the membership, including the number of temples or mosques (by then the two terms were used interchangeably) continued to grow, as did the Muhammad University of Islam schools associated with the temples/mosques. The NOI's primary communication and media organ, Muhammad Speaks newspaper, saw its sales volume increase dramatically, as did the overall financial and real estate holdings of the NOI; the fish import business was established, and many other successful economic ventures were instituted, all helping to actualize the often stated philosophy of Elijah Muhammad: *do for self*. By the time of his passing, it was estimated that under the auspices

45, 35, Now…..The Continuum of Islam in America

of the Nation of Islam, he built an empire worth more than 85 million dollars.

Just as important, from an ideological or organizational standpoint during this period, as it relates to the topic at hand, any of the late 1950s to early 1960s attempts at seeking to gain *Islamic legitimacy* in the eyes of immigrant Muslims or the Muslim world were a thing of the past. The Nation of Islam under the undisputed leadership of the man known to the world as the Honorable Elijah Muhammad remained a viable socio-religious entity and independent organization; one that was a powerful force to be reckoned with in what Elijah Muhammad dubbed *the wilderness of North America.*

It would take an entire decade, a few days past ten years from the assassination of Malcolm X, for the beginning of the transition of the Nation of Islam; a transition to a new Islamic ideology, one that would bring full circle the mission that began under the leadership of the man that Sandersville, GA produced in 1897.

45, 35, Now…..The Continuum of Islam in America

35: February 25, 1975 – The passing of Elijah Muhammad
October 7, 1897 – February 25, 1975

On February 25, 1975, the man known to his followers as *the Honorable Elijah Muhammad*, who had led the Nation of Islam since the 1930's, departed this life after suffering from congestive heart failure. He was 77.

The legacy of Elijah Muhammad and his work during the more than 40 year period that he served as architect and leader of the group formally known as *the Lost-Found Nation of Islam in the West*, is well documented. A number of works, biographies and historical narratives have been written. Arguably, the most popular of the earlier works is the classic text by the late seminal scholar C. Eric Lincoln titled the *Black Muslims in America*. Over the later decades would follow extensive works by Evanzz, Clegg and others.

Briefly, Elijah Muhammad was born Elijah Robert Poole, the sixth of thirteen children, in Sandersville, GA in 1897. His formal education ended at the fourth grade, as to help support the family he worked with his parents as a sharecropper. When he was 16 years old he left home and began working what would become a series of jobs, at factories, etc. In 1917 he

45, 35, Now.....The Continuum of Islam in America

married Clara Evans and they ultimately settled in Hamtramck, Michigan, where through the Great Depression, Poole struggled and worked hard to support his growing family. He and Clara would ultimately have eight children, six boys and two girls.

In 1931, and apparently at the urging of his wife who had attended previously, Poole attended a speech given by Wallace D. Fard, a man of then-unknown and mysterious origin who was, what was referred to as at the time, a silk peddler, as he went door to door through the city of Detroit selling his wares.

Oftentimes, he would talk about how the fine silks and garments that he sold were the same as what Black people wore in their original lands. He would use this analysis to form the basis of what was essentially the foundational doctrine of what would become the NOI, which was self-help and empowerment through "reclaiming your own".

After hearing Fard speak, Poole joined him in what would be then known as the *Allah Temple of Islam*, and became his most ardent student. His wife, brother and several others would also join, forming the early basis of the organization's membership. A series of events would ensue over the next few years, including a police investigation of a ritual murder, the arrest of Fard and his subsequent release and order to leave Detroit,

45, 35, Now…..The Continuum of Islam in America

which culminated in Fard's disappearance in 1934. He was succeeded by Poole, who had already by then, at Fard's request, changed his surname to Muhammad. It was also then that Elijah Muhammad told the remaining followers, now his own, that the man known as Wallace D. Fard was actually the presence of God on Earth. He would henceforth be referred to as Master Fard Muhammad.

After surviving a power struggle for the leadership, including a challenge from one of his brothers, Elijah Muhammad assumed control of the NOI which then consisted only of Temple No. 1 in Detroit. In 1935, Muhammad left Detroit and settled his family in Chicago. From there, he traveled to Milwaukee, Wisconsin, where he founded Temple No. 3, and then moved on to Washington, D.C., where he founded Temple No. 4. It is said that while there in DC, he spent much of his time studying at the Library of Congress.

On May 8, 1942, Elijah Muhammad was arrested for failure to register for the draft during World War II. After he was released on bail, Muhammad fled Washington D.C. on the advice of his attorney, and returned to Chicago. It was there that Muhammad was arrested and charged with eight counts of sedition for instructing his followers not to register for the draft or serve in the armed forces. Found guilty, Elijah Muhammad served four

45, 35, Now.....The Continuum of Islam in America

years, from 1942 to 1946, at the Federal Correctional Institution in Milan, Michigan. During that time, his wife Clara, along with a few trusted members, assumed responsibility for running the NOI. These trusted aides ran the organization and this continued until his release.

Following his return to Chicago, Elijah Muhammad continued his work in earnest of building the Nation of Islam. The organization had retained most of its modest membership level during his imprisonment, and its membership increased after his return. From four temples in 1946, the Nation of Islam grew to 15 by 1955. By 1959, concurrent with Malcolm X joining the NOI and a few years earlier and building upon the foundation that had been laid; the NOI consisted of 50 temples, with membership of various sizes, in 22 states.

As noted earlier, after Malcolm's departure from the NOI in 1964, by the 1970s, the Nation of Islam had established a business presence that would exceed any independent Black organization that existed; the NOI owned bakeries, barber shops, coffee shops, grocery stores, laundromats, a printing plant, retail stores, numerous real estate holdings, and a fleet of tractor trailers, plus farmland in several states including Alabama, Georgia and Michigan.

45, 35, Now…..The Continuum of Islam in America

In 1972 the Nation of Islam took controlling interest in a bank, the Guaranty Bank and Trust Co; that same year, it acquired its flagship mosque in Chicago, a beautiful, sprawling former Greek Orthodox church. The University of Islam continued to expand, and by 1975, there were schools in 47 cities throughout the United States. It can be stated that from an organization standpoint, Elijah Muhammad fulfilled much of his vision of *building a Nation*. And space does not allow for the endless personal narratives that can be provided of those who benefitted greatly from his work, having their lives altered in the most positive sense, which can account for the admiration and unwavering loyalty he received from his followers, I, a child at the time, being among them.

Of all the historic dates that I cover in this work it is this date, February 25, 1975, that has had the most profound impact upon my life. And although this is not a memoir, (that project is a work in progress and forthcoming, Allah willing) allow me to share with you my personal narrative of that day to help elucidate and better illustrate its profundity. I have shared this story in a previous writing as well as in many lectures over the years around the topic.

45, 35, Now…..The Continuum of Islam in America

It was mid-morning on Tuesday, February 25, 1975, and I was home in East Orange, New Jersey, eagerly anticipating the next day which would be *Saviour's Day*, the annual Nation of Islam national convention in commemoration of the birthday of its founder, who previously noted, was the mysterious peddler who appeared in Detroit, Michigan in 1930 named W. D. Fard, known and referred to in the Nation of Islam as Master Fard Muhammad. My parents had traveled to Chicago for the convention, as they normally did, like almost every member of the NOI who could possibly get there. I have been told, and know personally, the stories of some of the more, to put it mildly, *enthusiastic and zealous* members of the NOI who tried to walk to Chicago from New Jersey. One brother collapsed and passed out in his attempt to make the journey on foot, and legend has it he was found on Route 280 West, just where Route 80 begins. At least he was headed in the right direction.

Continuing with the narrative, I was at home with my younger sister and a Muslim woman, a dear sister who today I still refer to as my *aunt*. She attended the Elizabeth, New Jersey Mosque where my father served as Minister, after being under the tutelage of the late Minister James Shabazz, the head of Mosque #25 in Newark, NJ, known affectionately in Nation of Islam circles as "the Son of Thunder". Shabazz was assassinated in

45, 35, Now…..The Continuum of Islam in America

Newark, New Jersey, in the driveway of his home, on September 4, 1973, my mother's birthday. His murder was another of the key events that occurred during that pivotal 10 year period covered in the previous section.

In the midst of viewing television, our program was interrupted by a CBS news special report. Appearing on the screen from the new studio was respected journalist Walter Cronkite. Quoting him now to the best of my recollection, although as it was indelibly etched in my memory I believe it to be exact: "Elijah Muhammad, the leader of the Nation of Islam and the Black Muslims has died of congestive heart failure in Chicago. He was 77 years old." As he was giving his narrative behind him appeared a picture of the man who I thought was immortal. I do not remember if he said anything else after that, but the interrupted program resumed, but I remember a moment of complete silence as the dear sister and I just looked at each other.

My sister, who was only four years old, was oblivious to what was going on and of course continued with her routine. I however, just three weeks shy of my eleventh birthday, had a completely different reaction and response to Mr. Cronkite's special report. I immediately turned off the television, and as the dear sister looked at me, seemingly for reaction, (as a student of the University of Islam at the time I was known for being sort of what we would refer to in the NOI as a *young scientist*), I summarily shared with her my assessment (again, verbatim, from memory): "Sister, that's a lie! The Honorable Elijah Muhammad is not dead! That's nothing but the devil's propaganda, trying to divide our people the day before Saviour's Day!" I then assured her that I knew that my father would be calling soon and that he would confirm the truth for us that the Honorable Elijah Muhammad was not dead and that everything was alright.

As the story was being repeated over various other television networks, the telephone at our home began to ring continuously. Members of the NOI were calling each other all over the place in an attempt to make some sense of this story. Most of the people from our temple were calling to find out from the sister who was watching us if she or I had heard from my father who was already in Chicago. When my father called shortly thereafter, he told me what I heard was true. He told me that the Honorable Elijah Muhammad had died and that there would be a new leader who would lead "the Nation" and everything was alright. He said that I should prepare to go to Saviour's Day tomorrow and to stay strong. Hearing his voice that day gave

45, 35, Now…..The Continuum of Islam in America

me a lot of reassurance and I was able to get some rest that night, after what was for me, the days' tragic turn of events.

My father would later tell me that on that same evening, there was a meeting of laborers as they were referred to, specifically NOI ministers, captains and secretaries, where the new leader was introduced; he was the son of the Honorable Elijah Muhammad, the same son who in our home was in a picture with his father, where he was holding a copy of the Qur'an. Wallace D. Muhammad was now the leader of *the house that Elijah built.*

To close this section, what follows is the official statement issued by the Nation of Islam upon the death of Elijah Muhammad, unedited and exactly as printed in the March 14, 1975 issue of Muhammad Speaks newspaper. It read as follows:

The Nation of Islam issued the following statement, Tuesday Feb. 25, 1975 at 4:30 p.m. central daylight time:
The Muslims are heavy hearted because of the absence of our Leader, the most Honorable Elijah Muhammad. We offer these words of encouragement to His followers everywhere:
The Messenger taught us, we have five senses, but that no one sense can satisfy all the needs of the body. We should use all

45, 35, Now…..The Continuum of Islam in America

the senses working together. Now is the time the body must use all the senses and stay together.

The Messenger spent all His life in efforts to better the conditions of the Black man. We should try to see that we keep His principles and ideals in us. The loss of the Messenger's presence is a great loss. He worked for the unity of the Black man. It is a greater loss to lose His principles.

The Holy Quran teaches that we should not refer to the righteous as being dead.

The Messenger has returned to Allah. He lives on in His works, and more important, He lives on in us. His leadership remains.

That statement sets the stage for what would transpire the following day, February 26, 1975; the day that would change the course of Islam in America for the rest of the 20th Century, and beyond.

45, 35, Now…..The Continuum of Islam in America

February 26, 1975 – Wallace D. Muhammad becomes the leader of the Nation of Islam

On Wednesday, February 26, 1975, I was in Jersey City, NJ with over 3,000 other members and supporters of the NOI, mostly from the Northern New Jersey area. We watched the *Saviour's Day* proceedings via closed circuit television (for our younger readers, this was the technological predecessor to the *webcast*) at a movie theater that was rented out for the day. The mood was particularly somber on this occasion because everyone realized that Elijah Muhammad had died the day before. Remember that this was a person who we, young, old and in between, believed would live forever and that he would live and lead us "until the return of God Himself".

There was a feeling of uneasiness and doubt that day. The future of "our Nation" was at stake, and among those who did not know, especially the common rank and file NOI member, many rumors were floating around. Where was the Nation headed? Who would be the leader? Minister Louis Farrakhan, the then-National Representative? Minister Yusuf Shah of Temple No. 2 who was a personal assistant to Elijah Muhammad? Many possibilities were mentioned. Very soon,

45, 35, Now.....The Continuum of Islam in America

this would all be put to rest, definitively, unequivocally and unquestionably.

To begin the program, there was a mini-documentary film that highlighted the life and good works of Elijah Muhammad, a tribute film of sort. Throughout the film, which lasted a full two hours, you could hear the sobs throughout the theater. People were visibly grieving, some uncontrollably. I cried like never before, but in my heart I believed that Allah, as I understood him then, had a plan and that our Nation and our people would be alright. In all honesty, in my heart I believed at that time, again just short of age 11, that Minister Farrakhan was the logical choice to become the new leader. Of course, I felt that no one could ever replace or succeed the Honorable Elijah Muhammad, but I also believed that out of all the ministers and personalities in the NOI, no one had the charisma, was as articulate and could represent it better than Farrakhan.

As the National Representative for the past 10 years, he certainly had major visibility. He was on television, he was on the radio throughout the country and he had the good fortune of being based in the media capital of this country, New York City. My father had always spoken highly of Minister Farrakhan and they enjoyed a very close relationship. I had also

45, 35, Now…..The Continuum of Islam in America

met him personally, on a few occasions, and he always seemed confident, personable and dynamic. A natural leader I thought. My father would later tell me that it was pretty well known within the higher circles of the NOI that if anything would happen to Elijah Muhammad, his son Wallace would assume the leadership. In 1974, he had become more visible again and was "teaching" in various places throughout the country.

In any event, I watched and listened as the National Secretary, Abass Rassoull declared before a packed house of over 20,000 people at the Chicago Amphitheater and to hundreds of thousands of others watching on closed circuit television across the country, that the mantle of leadership of "the Nation" has been passed to Minister Wallace D. Muhammad. He would initially be referred to as the *Supreme Minister of the Nation of Islam*.

I remember clearly that my initial response was one of hesitation and unfamiliarity. I had to think hard for a moment to remember that I had heard of him before. Then, almost immediately, I recalled that he was the same son in the picture on the wall in our home. I also remembered thereafter that he had been in some trouble and had been excommunicated on a number of occasions.

45, 35, Now…..The Continuum of Islam in America

One by one, I watched as many of the NOI national officials and other personalities came forth to express their love for Elijah Muhammad, his family, referred to as *the Royal Family* and their support for the new leadership. They included Raymond Sharrieff, who was Elijah Muhammad's son-in-law and the head of the men's paramilitary group known as the Fruit of Islam (FOI) serving as Supreme Captain; Nathaniel Muhammad, one of Elijah Muhammad's sons who also served as a Minister; Jesse Jackson who was head of Operation Push, also based in Chicago; Muhammad Ali, who at that time was still the world's heavyweight boxing champion, and many others. I remember, while also being fully attentive, engaged and enthralled, this seemed to go on endlessly, like a parade.

The ministers from some of the largest temples in the country came forward to express their total, unwavering support. Minister Abdul Rahman of Temple #15 in Atlanta, Georgia, the NOI Southern powerbase, declared in his heavy southern accent "I pledge the South!" (Ironically, he ultimately followed Minister Louis Farrakhan when he left to reestablish the NOI and remains with him still). Minister Abdul Karriem of Temple #27 in Los Angeles, California, and many other influential ministers addressed the audience.

45, 35, Now…..The Continuum of Islam in America

Then Minister Farrakhan, after emotionally and emphatically extolling the virtues of Elijah Muhammad, with tears streaming down his face, he went on to pledge his support to the new leadership. He even went so far as to proclaim that "No one else holds the key to divinity! No one else's knowledge could even approach the shoelace of Wallace D. Muhammad!" Finally after Min. Farrakhan completed his comments, and after a few brief comments from Minister Jeremiah Shabazz of Temple #12 in Philadelphia, PA, the moment had arrived. The climax of the day's events; we would finally get to hear the new leader of the Nation of Islam, the Honorable Wallace D. Muhammad, Supreme Minister and Servant of Allah. This was his first official title as printed in the subsequent edition of Muhammad Speaks newspaper.

The room became filled with chants that had become common place at Saviour's Day and at other NOI rallies: "Long Live Muhammad. Long live Muhammad". The Supreme Minister gave a rousing speech, comprehensively acknowledging the life and works of his father, reading a section from the Islamic text, which he stated clearly is "our Bible, properly called the Qur'an". This would be the start of his transitioning the NOI into the concepts and language of the Qur'an, which before then had only been minimally referenced, and when it was, only

45, 35, Now…..The Continuum of Islam in America

mostly in support of NOI doctrine. In this speech he also deftly, yet firmly, addressed the need to stand on strength and knowledge, not on emotions. Among his comments, he stated "the winds of emotion will not shake or move even the curtains in this house". This apparently was a not so subtle reference to the emotional pleadings of Minister Farrakhan prior.

I remember how energized and reassured I felt after hearing the new leader speak; and I resolved at that moment that I would love him as I loved his father, and my mission would remain the same: be a good Muslim and keep soldiering as a *junior-FOI*, and at the age of 16 I would receive my rite of passage and be able to *soldier* as an FOI and help continue building our Nation. I had my life all planned out; just after my 16th birthday I would marry a Muslim woman, an *MGT*, and walk down the aisle, her in her beautiful white *longs* and me in my blue FOI uniform. She would be *beautiful* and know how to make bean soup, carrot loaf, gravy smothered baked chicken and all of that! And just like my parents, we would have our own *junior-Fruit* and *little MGT*. Little did I know what changes would lie ahead and what the future would hold. The Nation of Islam, and my life along with it, would be forever different. And surely Allah is the Best of Planners.

45, 35, Now…..The Continuum of Islam in America

The Second Resurrection begins

Almost immediately following his February 26, 1975 address, Imam W. Deen Mohammad, as he later came to be known, subsequently began a course of action that would significantly change the direction of the Nation of Islam from a mainly nationalist, social change organization with some of its concepts, ideologies and philosophies based upon and derived from Islam, to a community based upon the truth of Islam as revealed in the Qur'an and as exemplified in the life of the Prophet Muhammad, prayers and peace be upon him, known as *the Sunnah*.

As the religious ideology of the NOI was laden with concepts that were not consistent with the teachings and practice of Islam, there were major hurdles to overcome. Central to these ideologies was the myth of a man as god, a messenger coming after the Prophet Muhammad, a race of people being condemned as "devils", and other philosophies and teachings. Imam Mohammed began to strategically and systematically transition the NOI's core beliefs and practices. In addition, he also began to change the organizational structure that had previously existed for decades.

45, 35, Now…..The Continuum of Islam in America

Through both numerous public lectures, and extensive articles in *the Nation's* weekly newspaper, he set out on his theme that he outlined in a March 1975 address in Philadelphia, PA entitled *Remake the World*. I was with my father back stage after that address and I remember meeting him as he prepared to exit the arena and he came by and greeted us and smiled. I felt the same way I did when I saluted his father at the Muslim Day Parade in Chicago, 1970.

The new leader would began to introduce more and more concepts and terminology that were consistent and more in line with correct Islamic teachings. Particularly, emphasis began to be placed upon the five pillars of Islam, a distorted version of which we had previously learned in the NOI. Through a series of articles, many were exposed, some for the very first time, to the correct understanding of fundamental concepts, such as; the Oneness of Allah (Tauheed), Salat (prayer), Saum (fasting), Zakat (poor tax), and Hajj (pilgrimage to Mecca). By the end of the year, 1975, the Nation of Islam had begun to address all of the basic concepts of correct Islam. At the conclusion of the month of Ramadan that year, close to ten thousand (10,000) Muslims attended Eid ul-Fitr prayer at the mosque in Chicago. The next two years would prove to be particularly challenging.

45, 35, Now.....The Continuum of Islam in America

Continuing into 1976, the NOI continued the process of transition. This year would be the last Saviour's Day observation, and by the end of the year, even the name of the organization would be changed. *The Nation of Islam* would now be known as *The World Community of Islam in the West (WCIW)*.

Imam Mohammed changed his title from *Supreme Minister* to *Chief Minister*. The business holdings of the former *Nation* were restructured, with many debt-ridden businesses being sold or otherwise discontinued. The paramilitary structure, known as *the Fruit of Islam (F.O.I.)* was disbanded in an effort to create a more spiritual, balanced environment. The magnitude of the transition was enormous.

The changes that continued are too numerous to be mentioned in the space allowed, and much more extensive research has been and continues to be written documenting the historic transition. And although in 1977, Minister Louis Farrakhan, who had been renamed Abdul-Haleem Farrakhan and had worked along with Imam Mohammed to that point, left the organization and began to rebuild an organization based upon the original Nation of Islam model, (also to be known as *the Nation of Islam*) the transition continued unabated.

45, 35, Now…..The Continuum of Islam in America

It should also be emphasized that although more effective and immediate in some areas than in others, there was great success still. Today, the entity that evolved from the *Nation of Islam*, to the *World Community of Al-Islam in the West (WCIW)*, to, briefly, the *Muslim American Society (MAS)* then the *American Society of Muslims (ASM)* until August 31, 2003, and reformed then as the Mosque Cares – the Ministry of Imam W. Deen Mohammed, until his passing and continuing today, the group commonly referred to as *the Community in association with the leadership of Imam W. Deen Mohammed*, represents the largest segment of people of African-American descent to enter into the fold of Islam in the 1970's and 80's.

I assert, from my perspective having been amongst those whom by the grace of Allah was a part of and lived through that first transition, is that in spite of some problematic areas that may have existed, history will record this effort as one of great merit and of significant importance to the Islamic Experience in America and on the world scene as well.

45, 35, Now.....The Continuum of Islam in America

February 27, 2000 - Saviour's Day weekend and the public reunion of Imam W. Deen Mohammed and Minister Louis Farrakhan

"FAMILY! Min. Farrakhan and Imam Mohammed embrace at Saviors' Day 2000". This was the headline on the March 14, 2000 issue of the Final Call, the weekly newspaper of the Nation of Islam.

Since 1977, Minister Louis Farrakhan, known to his followers as the Honorable Minister Louis Farrakhan, has been at the helm of the Nation of Islam, reformulating the group in 1977, culminating with holding the first Saviours Day under his leadership in 1981. Under his leadership, many, if not all, of the concepts, ideologies, philosophies and teachings that had been eradicated during the transition that we have previously identified as did Imam Mohammed at the time, as *the Second Resurrection*, have been reclaimed and reinitiated. Now, on this day, twenty five years and a day since Imam Mohammad assumed the leadership of the then-Nation of Islam, and more than two decades since their last public appearance together, Farrakhan welcomed Imam Mohammed at the NOI's annual gathering still referred to as *Saviour's Day*, which is among the programs that he has resumed.

45, 35, Now…..The Continuum of Islam in America

Breaking the Ice

After decades of what could certainly be categorized as a strained relationship, the two would meet during this historic weekend, which included Jumu'ah prayer (Friday congregational prayer service), a tribute to the family of Elijah Muhammad, specifically, the siblings of Imam Mohammed born by his mother Sister Clara Mohammed, and many other activities and ceremonies. The weekend culminated with the Saviour's Day keynote address by Farrakhan, on February 27th, in front of twenty eight thousand (28,000) people at the United Center in Chicago, IL.

As reported in the Final Call newspaper, March 14, 2000 "The Imam and I will be together until death overtakes us and we will work together for the cause of Islam. We will work together for the establishment of Islam; not only among our people, but to establish Islam in the Americas", said Farrakhan. Continuing from the same edition of the Final Call "Allah (God) in the Holy Qur'an says Muslims are one community and should not be divided, and says that all human beings started from a single source, and will return to that source", said Imam Mohammed in his remarks prior to Farrakhan's keynote address.

45, 35, Now…..The Continuum of Islam in America

For many, this historic reunion of sorts signaled the beginning of Minister Farrakhan's fulfillment of an often promised, yet never realized transition. To some skeptics, his words were nothing more than just that; words. However, this year 2000 proclamation was particularly different from those made in the years past.

One, in the years following the reunion, Minister Farrakhan had continued to fight a much publicized, difficult battle with prostate cancer. On many occasions, he has commented in words to the effect upon how the reality of death makes you view things differently and certainly brings the meeting with your Lord into clearer focus. Many argued, *Islamic ideologically-wise,* that perhaps Minister Farrakhan has seen the proverbial light. What we do know to be a fact, based upon research and firsthand experience is that over the few years proceeding 2000, actually since the early 1990's, with increasing numbers, many people had begun the journey from the Nation of Islam under Farrakhan and to the path of traditional Islam, based upon the Qur'an and the Sunnah of the Prophet, prayers and peace be upon him.

At that time, the year 2000, throughout the country there had been reported increases in the frequency and number of people

45, 35, Now.....The Continuum of Islam in America

coming from the NOI to masajid (plural for mosques) and Islamic centers throughout America, particularly within the urban centers. This phenomenon is proving to be the norm and not an aberration. We know of many cases where people had recently left the NOI and made the shahadah, the Declaration of Faith in the form of a verbal statement that one makes to accept Islam: *There is nothing worthy of worship as a God except Allah, and Muhammad is the Messenger of Allah,* and are active, practicing Muslims within the tradition sense. Now, the window of opportunity had been opened, yet again, for another transition, albeit of smaller numbers, yet equally as important and significant, to begin in earnest.

The question that remained, and the challenge that awaited then, and that remains today, in light of the experience and wisdom gained from the first transition, was/is how would the bridge from *the Nation to the Sunnah* be effectively built in 21st Century America, continuing to contribute to the continuum of Islam in America? I had the pleasure of being with Imam Mohammad on Friday, March 3, 2000 at Harvard University where he delivered a beautiful Jumu'ah khutbah (the sermon that precedes the Friday Congregational Islamic Prayer). It was exactly one week after the Saviour's Day weekend reunion.

45, 35, Now…..The Continuum of Islam in America

We made eye contact as he entered the room, and as we smiled at each other (we had just been together late November 1999 in Newark where we shared dinner and almost two hours of excellent, heartfelt, revealing and certainly for me, enlightening and educational conversation), I immediately stood up to move towards him, and he broke away from those accompanying him, his security and several imams including my dear brother and colleague in the work, the late Imam Ali K. Muslim of Newark, NJ (may Allah have Mercy on him).

As we greeted each other and stood in the middle of the floor embracing, I could see he was energetic, almost jubilant. I asked him how he was doing, and his reply, exact words: "Alhamdulillah I'm fine. Imam Amin, we are back together again; we are all one family. Allahu Akbar!" I shared his enthusiasm, and we hugged again and he proceeded to prepare to give his sermon. I was with him again briefly after Jumu'ah before he departed Harvard. Before leaving, he told me that I, *we*, have to be available and ready to help the NOI as they intended to make and complete the transition. He knew that having already lived through it, perhaps *we* were best qualified, most uniquely positioned to help facilitate the process. I heard Imam Mohammed loud and clear; and I accepted my assignment without hesitation. I felt like *this* was how I was

45, 35, Now.....The Continuum of Islam in America

intended to *soldier* going forward. I subsequently had a conversation with my dear brother and mentor, Imam Siraj Wahhaj. He had been in communication with Imam Mohammad throughout, and shared his vision for, borrowing a popular NOI theme, "the time and what must be done" and how we could assist. He had already been in contact with the NOI minister in NY, who at the time was Benjamin Chavis-Muhammad, who formerly was head of the NAACP. He discussed with him how we could, and would, help instruct him and others he identified on the basic tenets of Islam, in preparation for their institutionalization of the five daily prayers, Jumu'ah and other activities and obligations in their respective mosques.

Unfortunately, save for a few attempts here and there, Philadelphia is one place I can personally speak with certainty of (Jumu'ah began, then ceased), the Islamization process never took hold at the local level. And at the national level, any widespread reform that may have been envisioned never materialized. I am privy to sources involved at the national level who have intimated that there is a divide of sorts among the *brain-trust* of the NOI leadership; ideologically speaking, you have one contingent that wants *change*, and another faction that does not; for varying reasons, much too in depth to begin to address in these pages. What I can state with certainty, based

45, 35, Now…..The Continuum of Islam in America

upon later future conversations I had with Imam W. Deen Mohammad, as well as through listening to some of his lectures etc., and an in depth interview he gave in 2007 where he expressed his total frustration with what he felt to be the lack of movement and progress on the part of the NOI towards an ideological transition, the February 2000 reunion and coming together that did not materialize in a full transition by the NOI was a source of disappointment and frustration for him.

He certainly saw this as an opportunity, a watershed moment to bring full circle the work he began after succeeding his father; work that he felt reflected the evolution his father was preparing the NOI for. Imam Mohammed expressed this sentiment, publically. I shared then, and continue to share now, that same disappointment.

As I will outline in the closing section of this book, my view, which I acknowledge may be controversial in some quarters, is that a movement built upon the correct understanding and practice of Islam based upon the Qur'an and the Prophetic tradition, with a practical application for 21st Century America, bolstered by the best practices of the economic, community engagement and organizational structure of the original NOI is a

45, 35, Now…..The Continuum of Islam in America

viable option for the Islamic experience in America; a new way forward for the 21st Century.

Now…..The Continuum of Islam in America

September 9, 2008 - The passing of
Imam W. Deen Mohammed
October 30, 1933 – September 9, 2008

On Tuesday, September 9, 2008, Imam W. Deen Mohammed, also known as Warith Deen Mohammed, departed this life at his home in Markham, Illinois. He was 74.

His *janaza* or Islamic funeral and burial, was held on Thursday, September 11, 2008 at the Islamic Foundation in Villa Park, Illinois and was attended by thousands, many who traveled from throughout the country and abroad. In addition to this service, across the country, there were numerous prayer and memorial programs held simultaneously at the time of his janaza. I was honored with the responsibility of leading one such program at the Philadelphia Masjid – Sister Clara Muhammad School.

The news of his passing sent shock waves throughout the Muslim community, America and around the world. *The Imam* as he was, and remains to be, affectionately referred to as, was a well known and respected figure nationally and internationally. I remember the sense of personal loss I felt when I received the

45, 35, Now.....The Continuum of Islam in America

news, which came as a total surprise, especially in light of his having just gave the public address at the annual Mosque Cares convention a few days prior.

There exists no autobiographical work on the life of Imam Mohammed. Even with all of his accomplishments and achievements throughout his 33plus years of leadership, at the time of his passing, his life was a true *work in progress*. My ardent hope is that the best of America's (and the worlds) academicians, historians, scholars and other social scientists, will produce volumes of biographical work that give his life and accomplishments the analysis and treatment they deserve. In the interim, I would direct the reader to the October 3, 2008 Special Edition of the *Muslim Journal Newspaper* (Volume 34, Number 1) and the subsequent two editions October 10 and 17, Volume 34, Numbers 2 and 3 respectively) for a brief yet outstanding overview of his life and work, including several timelines with key dates and milestones, along with pictorials.

In brief, the son of Elijah and Clara Muhammad, Imam W. Deen Mohammed was born Wallace Delaney Muhammad in Hamtramck, Michigan on October 30, 1933. Imam Mohammed grew up within the Nation of Islam where he also became a minister serving in Philadelphia in the late 1950s and the early

45, 35, Now…..The Continuum of Islam in America

1960s. He was excommunicated from the NOI on several occasions, for going against NOI doctrine and rejecting his father's teachings, particularly, the idea of the concept of Fard Muhammad as *God in the person*. In 1961 on his 28th birthday, he was imprisoned for refusal to serve in the United States military. During his 14 months in federal prison he spent most of his time studying the Qur'an, and while assessing the state of the NOI he became further convinced that it had to be reformed. In 1963 he was released from prison and continued to hope for the ideological and theological reform of the NOI. In 1965 after the assassination of Malcolm X, whom he considered as a friend, he was readmitted into the NOI. He continued to work to support his family and continued his study until 10 years later when he assumed the leadership of the NOI upon the death of his father.

As previously outlined, as the new leader of the NOI, Imam W. Deen Mohammed introduced many reforms and over time completely transformed the Nation of Islam, bringing it into the fold of mainstream Islam. In doing so, he rejected his father's theology and separatist views, as much of both were contrary to the tenets of Islam. In addition to allowing whites membership into the organization, his changing the name of the mosque in Harlem renaming it Masjid Malcolm Shabazz in honor of

45, 35, Now.....The Continuum of Islam in America

Malcolm X who established and led that mosque, was among his many monumental feats. He also forged closer ties with mainstream Muslim communities of all ethnicities. He was considered to be a foremost leader and advocate of interfaith cooperation speaking in numerous places throughout America and the world focusing on the commonality of the human spirit.

Throughout his more than three decades of leadership and service there are almost countless highlights and milestones of monumental and significant importance. Among the many: in 1977 he met with then President Jimmy Carter to discuss some of the crucial issues facing America, including drug addiction, immorality, senseless violence, and the problem of urban blight particularly in African-American communities. Over a decade later, in 1992, he gave the first invocation ever by a Muslim in the U.S. Senate. In that same year he became the first Muslim to deliver an address on the floor of the Georgia State legislature.

In October 1996 he met with (the late) Pope John Paul II at the Vatican in Rome; in October 1999 he returned again to Rome and addressed a gathering of 100,000 people at the Vatican with (the late) Pope John Paul II and the Dalai Lama in attendance. His legacy of accomplishments and accolades goes on and on.

45, 35, Now…..The Continuum of Islam in America

Again I recommend and refer you to the aforementioned *Muslim Journal* volumes for more dates and achievements.

At the time of his passing, Imam W. Deen Mohammed was the President of The Mosque Cares, the ministry and propagation initiative he began after formerly resigning as leader of the American Society of Muslims (ASM) on August 31, 2003. He also established and managed a business initiative called the CPC, or Collective Purchasing Conference. Through The Mosque Cares, he continued to travel throughout the country, speaking to and engaging Muslim audiences and interfaith gatherings. His articles and transcribed lectures were published weekly in the *Muslim Journal* and his audio and video recordings, along with his many books and other published works, remain available there. He had a syndicated television program, W. Deen Mohammed and Guests, broadcast locally and heard nationally in over 100 cities over the Internet. It was estimated that he has as many as 2 million followers or *students*, comprised of those that transitioned from the NOI and those who converted later, over the years of his leadership.

It can be accurately stated that Imam Mohammed meant and continues to mean many things to many people depending upon one's agenda, perspective or viewpoint. For some he was and

45, 35, Now.....The Continuum of Islam in America

remains a foremost scholar of Islam. For others, he was a reformer who began the transition process but did not venture far enough, in their estimation, to the *purity* of Islam and the Prophetic tradition. Again the volumes remain to be written based upon a critical and objective analysis of the life and works of Imam W. Deen Mohammed. Among his students, this work is already in progress. Certainly for his students, his analysis and exegesis of the Qur'an continue to provide keen insight into the meaning of Islam, particularly in terms of its application to life in contemporary society.

Having stated that, I have publicly stated that time and experience has allowed me to be more analytically objective and to see the importance and value of the philosophical approach of Imam W. Deen Mohammed. While some may view this as a recapitulation of some things I have expressed in a previous work, more than 16 years ago now, nevertheless, I state it here, for the public record.

In my first public statement after the passing of Imam Mohammed, including my Jumu'ah sermon in Irvington NJ, I stated, as I continue to do, borrowing from the statement of one of the Muslim community elders in Newark NJ: "Imam W. Deen Mohammed freed more slaves than Abraham Lincoln!".

45, 35, Now…..The Continuum of Islam in America

From an ideological standpoint, his work that began in 1975 freed those who followed him from the doctrine of the Nation of Islam. It allowed people to become free thinkers, not beholden to the concepts and practices that would be an impediment to the acceptance, embracing and practicing of *true* Islam. Another important contribution of Imam Mohammed, and this proved to be invaluable with the tragic events of September 11, 2001 and thereafter, is that he made it acceptable for a *Muslim* to embrace being an *American*.

In the Islamic experience in America, particularly that period concurrent with the Black Power movement, the tendency existed for many Muslims to demonize, denounce and shun all things deemed *American*. For some, claiming to be American was in some way diametrically opposed to Islam and being a Muslim. When it wasn't popular, and certainly far prior to September 11, 2001 and the political expediency that followed on the part of many within the Muslim community, Imam Mohammed embraced, and encouraged his followers, students and supporters to embrace their contribution and connection to America; the land that the ancestors of the African-American community help build. The DNA of our ancestors is embedded in the very soil and fabric that is *America*. Imam Mohammed, to the discomfort of many, took the lead and was the forerunner of

45, 35, Now.....The Continuum of Islam in America

the idea of *American Muslim*. The reality of 21st Century America would prove that his decision was prudent and in a word, visionary. I believe history and future historians will support and confirm this view.

I assert that the Muslim American community on a collective level has yet to realize the importance of the contribution and work of Imam W. Deen Mohammed, nor the void that his passing has left. I can vividly recall the many conversations I had with Imam Mohammed, beginning with the November 1999 dialogue over dinner that I alluded to previously, as well as future discussions that I have not mentioned. Some of them I intend to keep private, between him, me and certainly the Creator and Knower of All Things. Having stating that, I will assert that each exchange during the time I spent with him reinforced what I felt to be my mission and responsibility. In response to the questions that I asked, he gave me answers that provided the clarity I needed and enlightened me in a way that helped to greatly shape my growth and development into the 21st Century.

Most importantly, and I cannot overemphasize this point, he showed me that what might have been his language in 1975, 1980, or at other times, did not always reflect his language and

45, 35, Now…..The Continuum of Islam in America

commentary going forward. He brought the community through the transition in stages, at a level he felt was feasible, palatable and practical. Whether one agrees or disagrees with that approach, he should be admired and respected for that nonetheless. Certainly *the time and what must be done* dictates how and what we teach and implement, within the broad parameters of the religion of Islam. Often times it is *we* that have inserted the restrictions where they may not belong.

In the final section of this book, I hope to outline what I feel are some of the challenges that lie ahead along the journey which is the continuum of Islam in America, and how we can take the best of the lessons learned from the leadership and legacy of Imam W. Deen Mohammed from 1975 to 2008, and keep soldiering forward. Without his bold and courageous leadership and reform, I, like many others, perhaps would not be on the road we are upon today, by the permission of Allah.

May Allah, the One who Rewards all good works for His Sake, have Mercy on Imam W. Deen Mohammed, forgive him any shortcomings and grant him the Greatest Reward. Ameen.

45, 35, Now…..The Continuum of Islam in America

A New Way Forward for the 21st Century

What is important to note is that today, in 21st Century America, particularly with regards to continuing the work began by Imam W. Deen Mohammed in 1975, there exists much to make the bridge of transition more solid than before, thus helping to increase the potential for a successful one. The most important thing we have at our advantage is the gift of *history*. Malcolm X made a profound statement when he said:

"Of all of our studies, history is best qualified to reward our research".

Simply stated, we have the benefit of being able to do as the subtitle of this work suggests, *examining the evolution of the Islamic Experience……*; and in the transition that began in 1975, we have an accurate frame of reference to help us, in essence, access and evaluate methodologies and strategies, what works, what doesn't work and what is potentially problematic or questionable. As a community consisting of activists, educators, historians, leaders, thinkers, social scientists and the like, we should utilize this gift in our planning and strategizing.

Additionally, at our disposal is the very time that we live in. We live in what has been dubbed *"The Information Age"*. In

45, 35, Now…..The Continuum of Islam in America

addition to the Internet, which has revolutionized the way research is gathered and information disseminated, Islamically speaking, we have a wealth of material and resources available that certainly wasn't available during the first transition. Even for the English speaking person who doesn't understand Arabic, a multitude of educational and informative works have been published in English, and even Spanish, as many Latinos or Spanish Speaking Americans are also accepting Islam in increasing numbers.

Essential books, articles, journals, and other medium such as audio CDs, DVDs, computer software, etc., are available to help anyone interested in Islam gain a better working understanding of the religion and way of life. Another advantage that exists on the side of transition is the vast amount of masajid (mosques) and Islamic centers existing within the American landscape. The 2001 study that we mentioned in the introduction was from a random survey of more than twelve hundred (1,200) institutions, ranging from massive mosques and centers built from the ground up, to renovated storefront buildings and other such structures.

Other institutions where Islamic education can take place and information can be gathered and disseminated, such as da'wah

45, 35, Now.....The Continuum of Islam in America

(Islamic propagation) centers, college campuses, hospitals and the like, where often time Jumu'ah services and study circles are held, were not even included in the study. This illustrates that one literally has a multitude of resources to benefit and enhance the transition process, as well as the broader mission of *civic engagement and education* of the society at large. What now remains to be examined is how to best utilize the assets and tools at our disposal for the purpose of achieving our goal, in an intelligent, organized, systematic, and more importantly, *results-oriented* manner.

My view is that before any methodologies can be employed and any tools can be properly utilized, the first, most primary challenge is the task of *bridge building,* in two critical areas: the bridge between the *mainstream* Muslim community and the Nation of Islam, and between *bridging the gap* between the African-American and immigrant communities. This cannot be overstated, as it is of paramount importance.

Bridge Building: The Most Crucial Challenge – *From the Nation to the Sunnah,* **and between the** *Indigenous and Immigrant Muslims*

From the Nation to the Sunnah

It must be clearly understood that the Nation of Islam, both as it existed up until 1975, and as it still exists today in 21st Century America, has always been a hierarchical, highly organized entity. With this in mind, in order to effectively reach the masses still within the organization, a process must be developed and implemented to forge relationships for the sake of da'wah and engagement. First, an active effort must be made to reach the leadership within the organization, at even the local level. For many reasons, many rooted in the long legacy of slavery, it is understandable why the leadership of an established organization may be wary of the motives of those seeking to come and in effect, *lead* them.

Historically speaking, this view certainly holds merit, as the first transition was a witness to some attempts on the part of larger, *established* Islamic organizations, both within the United States and abroad, to "co-opt" the membership of the NOI in transition. In some cases, this resulted in what I describe as a *cultural and intellectual marginalization,* the effects of which are still being seen and experienced in our community in America today. Imam Mohammed became very resistant to this, although as his work continued, over time he was successful at forging stronger ties with some of the immigrant organizations while still remaining *organizationally independent*. This too was an important accomplishment.

It is a proven fact that people tend to gravitate towards the familiar, and as a result, especially in light of historic NOI pedagogy and orientation, those seen as erecting, standing on, or the other side of the bridge should ideally resemble those striving and yearning to cross that bridge. This view should not be viewed as racist, or nationalistic, or otherwise against the tenets of Islam. This is a matter of practicality, and even if one does an objective analysis of the da'wah strategies of the Prophet (pbuh) it is clear that he always sent among the people one of his Companions who understood their situation, culture, nuances, etc., and often times who was even what can be considered as from *among them*.

Following this example, and having the benefit of our own history of the transition in America at our disposal, it should also be clear that in order to effectively build this bridge, relationships must be developed first and foremost, between

Nation of Islam ministers (*now referred to as Student Ministers*), and Imams, Islamic workers and others engaged in the work of Islamic education and propagation. It has been established that the road to the masses is through the leadership, in most instances.

It must also be noted that as it relates to this transition, the term *Islamic education* means basic, practical, working knowledge, of course based upon Qur'an and Sunnah, yet enhanced by the reality of our situation in America today. Academic, or classical, scholastic knowledge has its place for certain, however, involvement at this stage of a beginning transition would be tantamount to sending one's child to college before they've successfully completed the prerequisite, preparatory education and schooling.

Towards a Comprehensive Strategy of Assimilation and Education

There are several important considerations to also factor in while attempting to build the bridge. As mentioned previously, some issues such as culture, ethnicity, familiarity and socio-economic status certainly must be considered in the transition process. This brings us to the issue of *assimilation*.

45, 35, Now.....The Continuum of Islam in America

Simply defined, this term means to be absorbed or made to resemble and be a part of the body, a larger group, etc. This is different and anti-thetical to *co-optioned*, which connotes to being absorbed to the point of marginalization, being rendered powerless and without recognition. At the very core of the NOI ideology is the idea of not feeling inferior to any race, creed, etc. In actuality, it promotes superiority over some races, which is anti-thetical to Islam, as illustrated in the Qur'an where it states (translated as):

Verily, the most honorable of you in the Sight of Allah is he who has At-Taqwa (piety, righteousness and consciousness of Allah). (Al-Hujurat - 49/13).

Therefore, in facilitating the transition, the educational process must include an effort to properly assimilate those making the transition into the mainstream of the Islamic community. This can be achieved through a broad and comprehensive education, one that takes a proactive approach and that will enable critical thinking. Most importantly, the people must be made to feel a part of the process, and not the demonized "other" simply because they may not yet possess the desired level of basic Islamic knowledge.

45, 35, Now…..The Continuum of Islam in America

In addition to the fundamental pillars of Islam, the articles of faith, and the other important spiritually based aspects, attention should also be given to Islamic history, proper Islamic *culturalization*, and similar issues aimed at ridding one, practically and intellectually, of any inferiority complex, weakness, dichotomy and lack of reality. Our strategy must also include the planning of a course of study that explains the goals, objectives and values of Islam, as a source of thought and culture, within a socially relevant context.

While embarking upon the process of learning and understanding the concept of tauheed, or the Oneness of the Creator, which effectively destroys any inferiority complex, we must use Islamic assimilation and education to help those making the transition and attempting to cross the bridge systematically, over time, purge themselves of all un-Islamic ideologies and philosophies.

Specifically, we are referring to the concepts that are contrary to the correct aqeedah, or creed, system of belief, and that would in the context of the Islamic criteria and definition, prevent one from being considered as a *Muslim*. The quest for inclusion is key, both on the part of the *transitioner* and those seeking to assist in helping with this process. To achieve this, we must

45, 35, Now…..The Continuum of Islam in America

wrap the vision around the methodology. 21st Century America presents us with enormous challenges and opportunities; yet, we have been provided with the vast resources needed to successfully achieve the task at hand. In addition to the resources which have been provided, I offer that what is needed most is cooperation and organization, on all levels.

Many efforts have been made, and are currently underway, to develop relationships for the purposes of da'wah and engagement between the mainstream Muslim community and the Nation of Islam. There are a few organizations I am aware of that are steadfastly working in this effort, both on a national level and locally, within the grassroots. However, even more needs to be done with respect to the national organizations. The rank and file of the Muslim community should implore all of the national organizations to work together and develop formal programs aimed toward the bridge building process for those seeking to make the transition, as well as for the good of Islamic da'wah in general.

Special mention must be made of some of the potentially problematic areas that still exist and remain. Many will say that as long as point number 12 of *What the Muslim Believes* still appears on the inside back page of the Final Call *(We believe*

45, 35, Now…..The Continuum of Islam in America

that Allah (God) appeared in the Person of Master Fard Muhammad…………) that there is no basis for dialogue between *us* and *them*. Until Minister Farrakhan publicly denounces his teacher, or at least that aspect of the NOI doctrine, we can never seek to bridge the gap with his organization.

My personal view is that this issue is greater and more important than Minister Farrakhan, and is certainly greater and more important than any individual or organization. It is about the responsibility that has placed upon us to help others as many of us were helped in coming from darkness into the light of Islam by whatever route we came. I assert the fact that the idol worshippers still worshipped their idols and committed the other atrocities consistent with their pagan way of life did not discourage or prevent the Prophet Muhammad (pbuh) from continuously, consistently inviting them to the Oneness of Islam, and to the Prophetic tradition and message.

Our collective duty, in spite of the challenges that may exist, both now and in the future, is to *invite*; **only Allah can *convert*.** The challenge is to remain steadfast, and do as the Prophet did for over twenty-three (23) years; deliver the message. If we collectively simply adhere to the responsibilities that have been placed upon us, and rise to meet the challenges, we will find that the mission of helping with the enormous transition from *the Nation* to *the Sunnah*, building the bridge in 21st Century America, and taking the lead in forging the road ahead which is the continuum of Islam in America, will be a vehicle by which the Muslim community is empowered to elevate, protect and uplift Islam. In doing so, we will be contributing to the improvement and salvation of humanity in the process.

Bridging the Gap Between Indigenous and Immigrant Muslims

The aftermath of the tragic events of September 11, 2001 bought to the forefront what for years in many circles had been the equivalent of the proverbial 800 pound gorilla in the room: the divide between the indigenous Muslims, particularly those of African-American descent, and immigrant Muslims. Much of what was being perceived by Muslim immigrants as a new and unprecedented assault on civil liberties is what had in most cases been the historical reality of many indigenous Muslims. As a result, the discourse had to begin to center on the source origin of the divide that exists between the two separate yet equal components of the same religious heritage.

The challenge that faces both the immigrant and indigenous Muslims of America, as cited by Yvonne Haddad and Jane

45, 35, Now…..The Continuum of Islam in America

Smith in their work *Muslim Communities in North America* is "how not to compromise the ideal unity in Islam while still maintaining some degree of ethnic identity and cultural affiliation."

I have argued for years now that of the many challenges from *within* facing the Islamic experience in America today, the development and nurturing of a relationship between the indigenous, particularly African-American and immigrant Muslim communities, based upon a foundation of mutual respect and an acknowledgement of different historical realities, is of among the most daunting and must be confronted. Only by meeting this challenge head on can perhaps this relationship be built, thus informing our present and future interactions. This will in turn build bridges of understanding while allowing for our respective cultural nuances and *particularisms*, all within the pale of Islam, within the broadest, most comprehensive context. To this end, the ultimate goal of Islamic community building, for the benefit of society-at-large, can become an attainable goal indeed.

In order to facilitate this open dialogue, we have to accept the fact that a gap truly does exist and acknowledge the reality of the challenges that the gap presents. Let us begin by defining

45, 35, Now…..The Continuum of Islam in America

two key terms. For this, I refer to The Oxford Dictionary, American Edition. *Indigenous* is defined as: 1. Originating naturally in a region. 2. (of people) born in a region. Native, local. *Immigrant* is defined as: 1. newcomer, migrant, settler, 2. (ethnic) minority, alien, foreigner.

These simple definitions help us to contextualize the two realities of "groups" that for the purposes of the discussion on the continuum of Islam in America, share one common link: Islam. All too often, one of the things that exist between the indigenous and immigrant communities is the adaptation of the familiar *us* and *them* mentality. In much of the private discourse that occurs, each group invariably refers to themselves as *us* (and *we*) and the other as *them* (and *they*).

In my analysis of the relationship, I have found that this is as a result of the different historical realities of both groups. This has proven to be a challenge for both sides and is an impediment to the attainment of true Muslim unity, more specifically, *functional unity*, as I have referred to it for some time now. As I noted in a previous work, all too often we find masajid, centers and organizations established and frequented upon ethnic lines. This often times has resulted in a duplication of efforts (for example, an *African-American* and an *immigrant* mosque within

45, 35, Now…..The Continuum of Islam in America

blocks of each other). Add this to the overall lack of mutual consultation on critical issues. This among other factors contributes to the climate of contempt and mistrust that is present on many levels.

From the perspective of a Muslim African-American, I offer the following historical considerations as a basis for why the Muslim African-American community is often sensitive to any perceived marginalization. Let's look at what occurred during the 2000 presidential election when a group of primarily immigrants presented themselves as "the Muslims of America" and endorsed then candidate and who went on to be elected president George W. Bush. As the indigenous people of the land, this endorsement, without the benefit of true shura or mutual consultation, was a source of alienization and disrespectful on many levels, albeit as unintentional as it may have been. And history and contemporary events clearly shows what "the Muslims of America" received over the eight years of that administration, especially post 9/11.

Fortunately, as America approached another presidential campaign and the subsequent election of Barack Obama in November 2008, more effort was being made to have diverse representation at the table where such major decisions as

45, 35, Now.....The Continuum of Islam in America

endorsements and the like, are usually debated and made. In the words of a man that was blessed to be truly ahead of his time, El-Hajj Malik Shabazz stated over 45 years ago, and it still rings true today: *"I'm not going to sit at the table and watch you eat and call myself a diner. In order for me to be a diner, I have to share in the meal."*

Referring to some historical facts that were noted earlier, I summarize the following for further consideration and reflection:

- Indigenous Muslims existed here in the US and throughout North America since the slavery period, starting around 1619 and ending in 1863.

- As many as 30% of all slaves introduced into the Americas from Africa in the 18th and 19th centuries were Muslims.

- Although Muslims from the Middle East began to migrate to the US in about 1875, the majority immigrated between 1947 and the mid 1960's, reflecting changing circumstances in Muslim countries.

- This wave of immigration led to the establishment of organizations and mosques in different parts of the US and Canada. The actual time of the first encounters between the immigrants and the indigenous African-Americans has not been well documented.

45, 35, Now…..The Continuum of Islam in America

- The evolution and continued development of the immigrant based organizations (i. e. MSA to ISNA, etc.) can be identified as one of the basis for the gap that exists, as there has traditionally been a lack of consistent indigenous representations within the leadership of these organizations.

- Thriving indigenous Muslim communities were developed throughout the first half of the 20th century, from as early as 1927. This trend continued and grew even more by the 1950's, into the 60's and 70's, concurrently with the existence of the Nation of Islam from 1930 until 1975.

- Even with the presence of many immigrant organizations, there was a major void in da'wah and correct representation of Islam in the United States. This void, along with the heightened awareness of African-American cultural identity, helped create the climate that allowed many prototype and pseudo Islamic movements and organizations to flourish.

These historical considerations should give one a greater appreciation of the Muslim African-American struggle and quest for self-determination. To further bring this into context, I present some additional historical considerations and recommendations for bridging the gap.

- As noted earlier, at least 33% of the estimated 7 to 8 million Muslims in America today are indigenous African-Americans.

45, 35, Now…..The Continuum of Islam in America

- The largest influx of indigenous Muslims entered into Islam with the beginning of the transformation of the Nation of Islam into a mainstream Islamic movement in 1975 and in the years that immediately followed. This cannot be overlooked, as it bears cultural implications of great magnitude.

For us to move forward as a united front through the continuum of Islam in 21st Century America indigenous and immigrants have to acknowledge what was stated earlier: we are both separate yet equal components of the same religious heritage and values. We have to fundamentally change the way that we deal with each other. We should commit to forming more effective collaborations, based upon mutual respect and consultation, in the establishment of organizations that endeavor to form a domestic-driven Muslim American agenda.

Much can be improved on both sides of the proverbial fence. History must inform what we do. We need to be more culturally sensitive to each other and respectful of the diversity of experiences. Not all African-Americans like fried chicken, and I'm certain that not all immigrants like biriyani. Just give me a choice. Anyone who has ever spent three days at a national convention knows exactly what I am referring to. I say that lightheartedly but as words for consideration as well.

45, 35, Now…..The Continuum of Islam in America

I can say that on a leadership level, within the national organizations, the discourse is continuing and much more is being done in the way of improving relations. I can envision one day that an African-American Muslim, man or woman, will one day be the *leader*, in more than a *figurehead* role, of one of the major traditionally immigrant led organizations. One might say who cares. Well, this is a far cry from the days of the past, in the mid 1970's where on a few occasions Muslim African-American students would picket and protest outside of major conventions because there was NO African-American presence on the leadership level whatsoever.

Our Muslim Community in America needs the active participation of both sides at the table if we are to effectively represent all of the Muslims in a broad and comprehensive manner. We can no longer afford to let either side be excluded or ostracized from making a contribution within all of our organizations, both nationally and locally. We need our best and brightest at the forefront, and we certainly find that we have been blessed with financial, human and social resources and capital on both sides. The gap can be closed, and any barrier that traditionally existed can and will be removed by our sincere effort towards that end.

45, 35, Now…..The Continuum of Islam in America

There are some very good examples of working relationships between indigenous and immigrant Muslims. And no pun intended, I can honestly say that some of my best friends in Islam are immigrant Muslims (as well as White Americans; yet another book subject). This is primarily due to the fact that we respect each other immensely.

They haven't adopted the proverbial spiritual big brother approach (you know the drill; we African-Americans are still *new* to Islam, so *they* will teach Islam and *we* will do maintenance and security….), and I haven't adopted the poor immigrant, contempt laced approach that we find sometimes exists in the Muslim African-American community. I have learned from them and they learned from me. We complement each other. This is what we all are supposed to do for one another as Muslims. We help to make each other better. This is not race specific. Sincere commitment and dedication, highlighted by knowledge is what makes us better, not race or ethnicity.

45, 35, Now.....The Continuum of Islam in America

Final Thoughts

As the year 2010 came to a close, thus turning the page on *45, 35*, a new year, 2011 began and I found myself reflecting more on the fierce urgency of now, and the current state of affairs of Islam and the Muslims in 21st Century America. As the month of Ramadan was fast approaching and I was working towards completion of this book with the goal of a September 2011 publication date, I began to feel overwhelmed when pondering the many challenges that face the Muslim Community of America. Add to this the reality of my own personal challenges, failings, insecurities and shortcomings, along with disappointments, tests and trials that are a companion and inevitable reality when undertaking the work of *leadership through service*, which is truly a labor of love, and I sometimes struggle to not become pessimistic.

Yet, I reflect upon my formative years in Islam, from the Nation to the Sunnah and continuing, all of those years included in the periods covered in this book, and I am reminded of just how far Islam and the Muslims in America have come. Upon completing this work I will resume writing my memoir of sorts; not because I feel as if my meager accomplishments and achievements merit such a work, but because in reflecting upon

45, 35, Now…..The Continuum of Islam in America

and reliving *45, 35, Now…..The Continuum of Islam in America - Examining the Evolution of the Islamic Experience in 21st Century America*, I totally agree with some of my friends and colleagues, among them a few academics, historians, researchers and social scientists in their own right, that the *personal narrative* is just as valuable as the *academic or scholarly study*. The narrative supports the study, and reflects for future generations to see, and for posterity, what was the thinking and thought processes of the time. A few of them have encouraged me for years now to document my own modest life journey and share it with *the world*; I have listened.

Until such time as that *work in progress* is completed, I continue to pray and search for answers, both about the direction my life will take going forward, and what role I can perhaps serve in this continuum, as well as the question I've posed in a previous work; *where do we go from here and how do we forge a new vision for Islam, a new way forward in 21st Century America?*

Again I am reminded of the quote by the psychiatrist and social theorist Frantz Fanon who said: "every generation rises from relative obscurity and either fulfills its historic mission or betrays it." I remain convinced now more than ever that it is the

45, 35, Now…..The Continuum of Islam in America

responsibility of those who have lived the journey of *from the Nation to the Sunnah* to play a significant role in shaping and implementing a new way forward that contributes to the continuum of Islam in America.

This is particularly so for those of my generation, those that witnessed the end of the NOI as we knew it in 1975, and are continuing our evolution, in some cases having children, even grandchildren (not me, yet!) of our own. This conviction informs and guides my thinking, planning and actions. And I emphatically assert that Muslims in America, at all levels, African American and immigrant, grass-roots *rank-and-file* and leaders and all in between, shoulder an enormous responsibility and it is incumbent upon us to commit ourselves to building the road for the future. Collectively, particularly at the grass roots level, we have a substantive contribution which remains to be made.

I refer to contemporary events and news and I'm reminded of the August 30, 2010 issue of Time magazine, with the cover story titled: *Is America Islamophobic?* In the feature story, we find revealing, yet troubling information and statistics, further illustrating how many Americans feel, and the misinformation and in many cases outright ignorance, about Islam and Muslims

45, 35, Now.....The Continuum of Islam in America

in America. Not so ironically it is in this article that the number of Muslims in the US is projected at a now lowly 2.5 million, significantly down from the numbers in this previously cited 2001 survey. I can cite the *Ground Zero* mosque controversy and a number of other contemporary events to illustrate that challenges do exist and much work remains to be done. However, we are already aware that the challenges will continue to exist and we are informed even in the Qur'an in the many places where we are told that human beings are tested in turn.

Throughout this journey which is the continuum of Islam in America I have come to categorize every test as part of the purification process, based upon the well-known adage "what doesn't kill you only serves to make you stronger." Islamophobia, blanket generalizations and judgments, sweeping stereotypes and other factors beyond our control may remain a constant; nevertheless we must not be thwarted and must remain unwavering in our endeavor to establish community life with the parallel pursuit of freedom, justice and equality.

For this vision to become a reality we must collectively seek common ground. This is one of the beauties of our historical development within the Islamic experience, particularly with

45, 35, Now…..The Continuum of Islam in America

respect to the title of this work. It is for this reason that I consistently reference my developmental years within the Nation of Islam, drawing from its best practices. The members of the NOI may have come from different backgrounds, neighborhoods, political ideologies, and socio-economic realities, etc., yet that shared NOI experience allowed the members to develop a certain trust and respect. It helped them to work through differences, staying focused on the task at hand and uniting to fulfill a common mission. In that experience, a precedence of *soldiering* together was established, and it was a labor of love, and as much as the common goal, objective and purpose then was to *build a nation.* I assert that the Muslim Community needs a common goal now to manifest a new vision for Islam and community life in 21st Century America.

In the process, our endeavors and collective work will allow us to accurately define for the broader society just what is *Islam* and to essentially redefine what it means to be a *Muslim.* The areas of engagement are multifaceted and multipronged, yet I firmly believe that for a new vision of Islam to be manifest at the highest level, an *Islamic movement* must commence. I am convinced that organizationally we have to move our collective work away from the institutional paradigm of loosely based alliances, organizations and the like. While those organizational

45, 35, Now…..The Continuum of Islam in America

modalities serve an important role, the sheer nature of our organized and collective work, for me, mandates that we solidify ourselves on a deeper level. When I use the term *Islamic movement*, I utilize the definition of one scholar I read who defines it as *organized and collective work that is undertaken by the people to restore Islam to the leadership of society and to the helm of life*. Of course, this Islamic leadership is accommodating and tolerant of other faith traditions, and it seeks inclusion, not exclusion, with morality and the pursuit of the common good serving as the true litmus test. I also argue that it is this type of movement, utilizing the best practices of the Nation of Islam, many of them from an administrative and organizational modality and standpoint, with a correct understanding and practice of Islam, with a practical application for 21st Century, is a viable option and a path worth venturing upon. Together, we can determine exactly what that looks like; I have some ideas and thoughts; and Allah certainly knows Best.

In shaping a new vision for Islam in 21st Century America and determining where we go from here, one must always keep in mind that the time dictates what must be done. You may be doing the right thing at the wrong time, looking for the right results. Our own collective assessment should help us determine

45, 35, Now…..The Continuum of Islam in America

what our challenges are and what the responses to those challenges should be. This requires us to discard with the proverbial slave mind. It is this mindset that keeps us waiting for the six o'clock news, and tuning into the popular culture to determine what our issues are and what our goals, objectives and priorities should be today. This is just one of many obstacles to taking control of our own destinies and developing and implementing a vision for the future.

We must be bold and courageous enough to chart our own course, always keeping in mind, particularly within a socio-political context, that they are no permanent friends or permanent enemies, only permanent interests. The interests that best benefit the overall aspirations of the community are those interests that should be a priority for our collective efforts, endeavors and struggle.

I personally do not separate my vision for Islam from my vision for America, as I am a Muslim and just as much an American. The blood of my ancestors is embedded in the soil of this land. Their sweat and labor helped to build the very country in which we live today, one that we have a vested interest in its vision, success or lack thereof. Again, I strongly believe that the religion and way of life of Islam, based upon a broad and

45, 35, Now.....The Continuum of Islam in America

comprehensive understanding with a practical application, can address many of the challenges issues and ills that exist in 21st Century America. Yet I also understand, as did Malcolm, and certainly Imam W. Deen Mohammed, that the challenges that face America are not Muslim, Christian or Jewish problems, they are human problems. Accepting and embracing this will be a significant step in regaining our social capital, particularly in the African-American community, which I feel, sadly, that we squandered during the transition. It is *there* for us to reclaim it. The people and the society are looking for leaders; all we have to do is *lead.* And to lead is to serve.

The time has come that we move beyond the manifestation of these problems and start examining and having discourse around the sources of these problems. And we can no longer be in denial, tiptoeing or soft-pedaling around our situation as it is too critical. The events of September 11, 2001, or "9/11" have grounded post modernity. That was our defining moment in the history of our generation. This reality has to move us to a more ecumenical co-existence.

I believe the first quarter of the 21st Century will be the most pivotal period in history; future generations will look back upon this period and we will be evaluated accordingly based upon our

45, 35, Now…..The Continuum of Islam in America

efforts and success or lack thereof, during this period. Like it or not, we are going to be history makers, the only question that remains is what kind of history will we make. The challenge is to address our issues and *fix ourselves* so that we can move *beyond ourselves*.

To manifest a new vision for Islam in America, and fulfill our collective destiny, our leaders, Muslim and other faith traditions, must move throughout our communities, throughout the country and convene with our people, the grassroots. We must all be on the same team and we can never make the tragic mistake of giving the ball to people who are playing for the *other* team. I define the *other* team as those who do not share in the goals, hopes and aspirations that will make us successful as a grassroots community in 21st century America.

I pray that I can help the *home team* and make a meaningful contribution to this new vision, a vision of hope, promise, success, and a fulfilled destiny, for the grassroots, and all of humanity.

My closing words are taken directly from a passage in the Qur'an, as this verse represents my personal mantra. I, as did many others, learned this prayer in the Nation of Islam; we said it every day. I knew little about *Islam,* as understood and practiced today, then, yet I never doubted the words contained in this prayer. So after *45, 35,* and living in the *now*, how could I ever doubt its importance, meaning and promise, today?

Surely my prayers and my sacrifice, my life and my death, are all for Allah, Lord of All the Worlds. No partners does He have, of this I am commanded; and I am the first of those who bow to His Will. (An'am 6/162-163)

My sincere hope and prayer is that we will all collectively embrace and implement the essence of these words in our lives as we forge ahead, and continue to *live* and thrive in the continuum of Islam in America, blazing a trail of hope and optimism and opportunity in the 21st Century.

About the Author

Amin Nathari is widely acknowledged as a critically acclaimed author, lecturer and commentator, as well as one of the leading and most passionate voices of his generation on the contemporary socio-political issues of our time. Nathari specializes primarily in the analysis and documentation of events and issues that impact Muslims and the Islamic experience in America today. He is also a renowned and respected activist and leader in the Muslim American community.

Nathari is the author of several books, including *A Message to the Grassroots for 21st Century America - What Would Malcolm Do?* (2nd edition printing September 2010, originally published 2008), *Muslim Unity By Any Means Necessary* (2004) and *Da'wah – the Invitation to Islam in 21st Century America* (2001). Additionally, Nathari is working on his memoir, tentatively titled *Going Back to Move Forward – My Life So Far (Growing Up Black and Muslim in America)* which is anticipated to be published in spring 2012.

For a complete biography, or any additional information, please visit www.aminnathari.com

45, 35, Now…..The Continuum of Islam in America

About IAM – the Islam in America Movement

Islam in America Movement (IAM) is a national organization-based movement founded primarily to help empower, strengthen and support the various *results-oriented* initiatives and projects of indigenous Muslims throughout the United States, particularly within the African-American community. Amin Nathari serves as the National Representative of the organization.

IAM is working to contribute to the development of a multi-faceted agenda for the Muslim Community in order to implement a comprehensive *domestic program agenda* and to empower Blackamericans as full participants in the development of Islam in America, while also working in cooperation and mutual consultation with the *immigrant* community.

Among the activities, programs and services and under development by IAM:

• *Institute for Civic Engagement (ICE)* - a national information and propagation (*da'wah*) initiative aimed at providing a clear and balanced representation of Islam and Muslims in America to the society at large, with a special focus on college and university campuses, as well as the media, both major and independent. In association with Sabree Press, ICE is also involved in various book publishing projects on a variety of socio-contemporary issues and topics. Additionally, ICE is preparing to serve as a *media response and resource center*, providing analysis and commentary to media outlets on the contemporary issues often covered in American and global media outlets, as well as offering media and communications services to Muslim communities.

- *Making It Plain with Amin Nathari (MIP)* - in association with NOW Media, a weekly internet broadcast, in talk show format, discussing the challenges and opportunities facing us today, in a language that all can understand. The show will feature special guests, including but not limited to, activists, authors, educators, entrepreneurs, scholars, social work and human service professionals and many others who are actively involved and making a contribution within the American landscape, from 'youth to elders". MIP is scheduled to launch in the fall 2011.

Founded July 4, 2008 in Philadelphia, PA and after three years of assessment, consultation, organizational development, planning and preparation, the movement is officially launching in the fall of 2011 with the introduction of *The Ten (10) Point Plan for Enhancing the Islamic Experience in America.*

45, 35, Now…..The Continuum of Islam in America

There are currently plans underway for a historic *Million Muslim March*, to be convened by Nathari and IAM, on Saturday, October 6, 2012 in Washington, DC.